Surviving Dementia

By

Emma Winter

This book was written in loving memory of my mum Val.
It was a way to recover and ease the pain from seeing her journey through the horrible illness that is Dementia. Hopefully this will help other families who have walked the same path and anyone who is just starting out on that journey themselves or holding the hand of a loved one.

It is also a thank you to my sister Louise for being there with me every step of the way and our families too, who helped us with our pain. Jack and lewis our son's and our husbands Andrew and Paul who we would have been lost without.

1. Finding Out!

I would prefer to say that our world was devastated by a huge bang and explosion and that we lost our mum and we were able to grieve immediately but unfortunately Dementia doesn't really allow you that blessing. It is more a confirmation of a growing worry and an initial damp squib in the realms of horrendous diagnoses, that confirms that worry. This grows daily into the horrendous reality of what Dementia has in store for you as a family from that point on.

My mum, our family lynch pin, was formally diagnosed with advanced Vascular Dementia on 28th May 2019. Also present on the scan was scaring of at least 2-3 small TIA's (Transient Isemic Attacks), otherwise known as a mini-stroke.

My sister and I were with her at the GP's after struggling over a few years to get her and my dad to acknowledge an issue with her memory. But the actual formal diagnosis was very much a formality and the access point to help rather than us being blown out of the water with shock. We unfortunately knew what was coming or we thought we did but you never can actually pre-empt what Dementia brings to the party! Mum was unfortunately beyond the point of medication to help slow or restrict the progress and symptoms of the disease in any way.

The prognosis of the disease, dependant on when diagnosis occurs, is terminal and gives the sufferer between 3-5 years before the number of strokes will end their life. We knew we were probably a long way on this path already, but it still felt horrendous to know that this person, our mum, would eventually physically leave us within that timeframe. The thing that we could never envisage was how mentally and emotionally we would be mourning our mum before she would ever pass. You are left caring for the husk of a person, who means the world to you but you no longer recognise. This is the basic reality of Dementia but actually living and dealing with Dementia as a family is so much more. Every tiny detail of life of the whole family is affected and it is utterly decimating in so many ways.

In this book I want to show a little of mums character and how we grew up with her showing her life's and loves and how she changed due to an illness which also changed all these aspects whilst leaving other things as a constant. How this disease affected us as individuals and as a family.

2. What is Dementia

Dementia is a disease that is greatly misunderstood by many until you are knee deep in dealing with it, that is. Some people feel it is an inevitable part of ageing and just forgetfulness but it absolutely is not. And I cannot say that loudly enough! Alzheimer's disease is the biggest cause of Dementia. Your brain is attacked and the brain cells are gradually damaged and destroyed. This can cause a variety of symptoms, generally gradually impacting on the person's life in many different way, which in turn impact on their loved ones as they try to fathom what is happening. It changes behaviours, functions, personality, emotions, responses and even memories to name a few. I experienced them all, we as a family experienced them all. Because of the damage done by Alzheimer's, people who suffer from Dementia have a brain that physically weighs 140g less than a healthy brain.

Some of the potential signs of Dementia I have listed below but these aren't exhaustive and always, always get medical help if you think a loved one is suffering with signs because if it is diagnosed the earlier the help is obtained the better for the sufferer, which in turn is better for you all as a family.

- Forgetting important dates, such as birthdays of children or loved one and repeatedly asking for the information on these.
- Relying on family to remind or do everyday tasks for them. Like taking medication or rotating food in fridges and cupboards.
- Struggling to be able to maintain or join in conversations or struggling to find a multitude of words or trailing off mid sentence.
- Putting everyday items such as teeth, purses, keys in incredibly unusual places and repeatedly doing this.

- Regularly losing items or indeed getting lost themselves especially in places that are unfamiliar or may have become unfamiliar due to changes
- Poor judgement or decision making which is out of character for that person and so is noticed by others, probably by people outside the family too.
- Regular changes to a persons mood and personality. This means they could appear to overreact to certain things that would not warrant that response or not respond to something that they would really have a response to. They could also become easily confused by things, very suspicious of people and what they are doing and why they are doing it. They may appear to be depressed or showing what appear to be symptoms of depression. They may be fearful in situations that have previously been normal situations for them.
- All of these things can lead to the

person becoming overly anxious and aggressive against their usual character or indeed withdrawn when they have previously been more outgoing.

I have compared this to the normal ageing signs that most people will experience at some point in their life.

- Sometimes for getting important appointments or names but remembering them at a later point.
- Sometimes forgetting a word mid conversation but again remembering later, within minutes or longer but remembering it later.
- Forgetting where you parked your car, or left your purse or glasses occasionally
- Making bad decisions at times but realising at a later point.
- Becoming irritable or withdrawn now and then when situations overwhelm or disrupt you from

your usual routine or plans.

So as you can see, looking at these symptoms side by side we will all have a bad memory or be a bit grumpy at times because we are humans and our bodies are ageing. But if you are generally fit and well, eat well, keep yourself physically and mentally active that is exactly what it is, an occasional lapse. Dementia is whole new and consistent level of differences. It is also possible to have more than one type of Dementia and so different symptoms that are more relevant to individual types can show. So it's really important to speak to Dementia specialists to not only ensure that the person suffering gets the right help but also family get the right help and advice going forward too.

Where do you go if you are worried about yourself or a loved one. The simple answer is the GP is your first port of call to discuss your symptoms as other things can contribute to memory issues and minor personality changes, especially in the very elderly, like water infections. So initially go to the GP and discuss things. They will then likely send you to see a specialist memory practitioner or to a memory clinic. Here you will be asked questions which will involve memory tests and also complete thinking tests. You will also have blood tests and brain scans to help complete the full picture and understand your specific type of problem. Again I have to say early diagnosis is always more helpful because it means you have more treatments available to you. Being an ostrich helps no one and just makes the whole situation so much worse and more painful.

I know one of my main worries following my mums diagnosis was that it would be hereditary, and that will bother many people but there is only a really small percentage of the many sufferers of this disease that will suffer from the type that is hereditary.

Genetic forms of Dementia, which are the hereditary types only accounted for I think 1% of cases when mum was diagnosed so it really is incredibly small.

To reduce your chances of developing dementia avoiding smoking. This is one of the biggest things and keep drinking down to below the recommended 14 units a week and avoid drinking all these units in one go. Eat well and look after your heart by eating a balanced diet and exercise regularly, at least 30 minutes 5 days a week. Also keep your brain as active as your body, read books, play games especially word games or maths problems or multiple sense games and problem solving. Get the family involved and have games nights. Make it fun with family and friends and you make memories too. And of course one of the big ones, try and keep stress to a minimum because it really does make a chemical difference to the brain not to have stress hormones in it all the time. This one always makes me roll my eyes out loud to be honest though because as we went down the rollercoaster path, it was one of the most stressful times in history. But it really helps both parties to keep stress down so do anything you can to achieve it.

The other thing to remember is that if you do get the worst diagnosis and a loved one has dementia it is not the end of the world. They can still lead a useful, full and happy life but they may and you as family may just need help. So get as much help as you can. I've listed places to go for help

- Your GP (remember you can talk to your GP for advise if your worried about someone)
- Your local Social `services. They have processes and avenues to help those suffering from the disease but also ways to help carers and prevent burnout for them.
- Alzheimers society Dementia

Connect – 0333 150 3456
- Age UK Advice Line – 0800 678 1602
- Independent Age Helpline – 0800 319 6789
- Dementia UK's Admiral Nurse Dementia Helpline – 0800 888 6678
- Carers Direct Helpline – 0300 123 1053
- Carers UK Helpline – 0800 808 7777
- www.nhs.uk have a list of many more online communities in local areas and nationally.
- Dementia Cafe's also help as drop in centres to give advice and just be among people who understand.

My other piece of advice would be get cleaners, gardeners, odd-job people, finance advisers, etc in place if you can so that you can remain as partners, friends or children of the person diagnosed and don't end up doing everything for them and being everything else and not having time to spend with them because your doing all the jobs. Also sort out a Power of Attorney so that you can act for that person, if it would be you, if and when you need to. You need to be able to be who you are with them and not be the head cook, cleaner, gardener, bottle washer etc as you'll be heading for upset, stress and tears.

3. Lets start at the beginning

Mum was born in South Elmsall, near Pontefract in South Yorkshire and lived most of her life in Hemsworth, a neighbouring village for most of her childhood and early years. It was quite a small mining village, where Grandad was the manager of The Thrift Stores, the initial Safeway's Supermarket. The first 5 years of her life Grandad was fighting in the second world war in Burma but he thankfully came home well and safe to my Grandma and mum. Grandad and Grandma were methodists and participated in the life of the local methodist church, bringing mum up to participate too. Unfortunately when mum was 13 years old my Grandma had a very large stroke and ended up a semi-invalid and there was very little help available so Grandad had to remain at work and mum had to care for Grandma in between school. Unfortunately, due to very little help that they received mum had a nervous breakdown at the age of 19 and finally they received some help. Mum was an amazing athlete as well during this time and competed at athletics especially the hurdles at Yorkshire level. She had to retire at 19 due to arthritis beginning in her hip joints. She also followed football and cricket with a passion and this would be a lifetime love.

Mum attended her local schools and became a prefect at her local Hemsworth High School but was never a lover of maths, in fact one teacher said that "Valerie has decided she cannot do maths" and yet she ran a household amazingly just on dads wage and helped dad run his business for over 40 years. She was perfectly able she just didn't like it. These snippets give you an insight into mums character. She was strong and determined individual and would give her all to her passions whilst tolerating other things with manners but they were in no uncertainty as to her thoughts about them. This was an absolute constant throughout her life even at her worst with dementia. She was very black and white in the rights and wrongs of life and we were brought up in a very moral way. Due to mums disappointment in the churches behaviour and help for her mum we were never brought up religiously. Mum regarded the fact that someone who had given her all to something and was then ignored by that same group that was meant to care as a core belief, as a moral disgrace. But we were given the chance to go if we wanted, I never felt the urge myself but agreed wholeheartedly with mums moral compass on behaviour and care of others and I know my sister does too.

When mum left school she trained as a hairdresser and worked in Wakefield as the manageress of a salon next to a cafe where dad used to go for a cuppa and dinner with his workmates. Dad was a heating engineer and gas fitter and took a fancy to mum straight away but wouldn't do anything about it other than chat to her as she was engaged to someone else. When he found out mum had broken the engagement off due to her fiancé's infidelity, not a good thing in the late 50's early 60's in a parochial village like Hemsworth, my dad swooped and took her out for a cuppa and to look at some boots he wanted to buy. And that, as they say, was that. Mum and dad adored each other and were married a year later and were together from March 1967 when they married until my dads death on 20th January 2020. They promised to look after each other completely and they did until dad passed with mum holding his hand as always.

4. Our mum and us growing up

Wow! Mum was a tigress as a mum and as a wife. We were very loved and very much wanted but we were always expected to play by the rules and we were never in doubt of our boundaries and that we were in trouble if we crossed a boundary line. If looks could kill......as the saying goes, was probably made for our mum! She could turn you to stone with one glance if you weren't behaving but she loved us so much and would defend us to the ends of the earth. She would however, even in your defence, make sure you knew what she thought. If she was your friend she would always be there with loyalty, time, love and give you her last penny and shirt off her back but if you crossed her and did that more than once she was no one's fool and you would be in no doubt where you stood either. She was black and white but thankfully she was our mum and she had our backs always.

I remember my sister being bullied on her way to school by an older boy and eventually when mum got out of her what was wrong she sent my sister off to school and told her not to worry as it wouldn't happen again. She waited behind the wall at the end of our street until the said boy went past. Mum located the scruff off his shirt and whispered in his ear that he better not touch her again or he would be in the biggest trouble of his life and not surprisingly he never did. We never knew this until many years after but the boy was known as one of the naughty tough boys who people dreaded being on the wrong side of but he never came near my sister or me ever again. Actions that today would be frowned upon possibly but in the 70's were definitely standard procedure.

I was once and only once sent home from school, in my final year of high school, by my head of year, 3 weeks before I left for good. My shirt had a little white embroidery flower on the collar of the white shirt. The head of year was spoiling for a fight, I could tell but I explained I had worn the shirt since the first year and had never been told it was unacceptable in 5 years.

I wasn't a tall child and am not a tall adult and mum always bought clothes for us to 'grow into'. He told me I was a liar and to go home and not to return until it was changed. I was mortified as nothing like this had ever happened before and I dreaded going home as mum was a stay at home mum and I knew she would be there. I knew I would be in trouble for teachers having had a cause to speak to me but knew I had to change the shirt to go back to school.

The picture of my mum on her hands and knees washing the kitchen floor as I walked in is as clear in my mind now as it was then. She looked up and said "are you poorly love?". (We had to be practically deceased to have time off school!) So I stood in the doorway, tears rolling down my face as I explained and told mum I'd been sent home because of my shirt and also called a liar. She took in a huge breath in and huffed and took off her pinny, that always meant trouble, and picked up her coat. She turned me round "Get yourself back to school" she said, "I'm coming with you and you wont be changing that shirt either!"

My heart was beating that hard it was like a thunder storm as we marched back to school. The receptionist asked for mums name as she asked for the teacher I had named and where he was. Her reply was that he will know soon enough and walked past her towards his office. The poor woman stood no chance against that force of nature. I was told to sit outside and believe me I did and did not move a muscle other than my stomach going round like a washing machine, which I could not quiet. I could hear mums very polite but very stern voice telling the head of year that what I had told him was true and she did not bring her children up to be liars and as such I would not be changing my shirt unless he wanted to put his hand in his pocket for a new shirt as I would be leaving school for college in three weeks and she and my dad were not made of money to buy clothes willy nilly to satisfy teachers whims.

I never heard his reply but she came out with him and he told me to go to class and mum nodded at me reassuringly and said "bye love. Ill see you at tea time". That shirt was washed by hand, dried and pressed every night for three weeks by my mum and I wore it every day until I left school. She definitely made her point and I was so grateful she had my back and very in awe of her and her strength at that time.

Mum tried to learn to drive when she was younger which was more unusual in those days but due to her nervous state when driving she refused to continue. And I say refused to continue rather than gave up as that is what she decided to do. She felt she didn't need to drive and cause herself stress therefore she felt no need to put herself through this and carry on. Anyway as we grew up myself and my sister got everywhere with mum by walking or on the bus. If dad was home he would take us, even to ballet and gymnastics, he never cared what people thought of him stood with a pink dance bag. He was a dad ahead of his time really. But it was generally mum. Anyway on holiday one day up in the Yorkshire Moors on the way back from Whitby, dad was driving our camper van back to our campsite and mum said "Oooh it's so quiet here that even I could learn to drive I think". Without hesitation dad pulled over and told her to get in the driving seat. He guided her calmly through the engine start up and gears and off we set with mum driving, back to our campsite back at Rosedale Abbey. Both me and my sister sat wide eyed and silent like startled rabbits but mum drove us back. Im going to gloss over the fact of no "L" plates but from that point on mum learnt to drive legally and we then were driven by mum. Until she reached 70. she then decided to stop, and stop she did, dad didn't want her to and I chatted to her as to why and she said she just had decided that things were too busy and she didn't want to and that was that. The line was drawn firmly in the sand. Dad was her strength and she his.

While we are on the subject of camping holidays we had the most magnificent tent. We glamped well before glamping was even a thing! We had a 6 berth tent, a room for mum and dad, a room for me and my sister to share and a room for the clothes on a hanging rail and the cool box for food etc.
We had a table, and a cooker inside the tent. Mum had collected carpet samples that the carpet shops gave away in those days and had sewn them together to create a fitted carpet. We took our shoes off outside, so we didn't fetch mud in, and these were placed in a weather proof box. Two groundsheets under the tent to prevent us getting cold and mum had a carpet sweeper to keep that carpet spotless. It sounds like insanity now

and it certainly did at the time to people who were onlookers but she was a woman before her time and had little care for others ideas on cleanliness and home making to be honest. Look at the glamping now and we were doing it in 1975. Standards were standards after all and just because we were in a tent did not mean we were going to live like feral animals in my mums opinion. Standards were things to be kept and kept consistently.

We made many many friends when we camped. Some who are still friends to this day. Who have been phenomenally supportive throughout mum and dads health issues and beyond. We rarely wanted to leave the campsites we stayed on for days out. We wanted to play with our friends, spend time in the river on rope swings, playing cricket on the playing fields, horse riding. One such evening mum and dad were playing cricket with us on the playing field at the Rosedale Abbey campsite, near

Pickering. Our family were playing with our friends family, who we met on this camp site, the Waites, when two young children asked if they could play with us too. Mum as always was utterly inclusive with all kids and said of course get yourself fielding and you can be the next bat. Mum had been an only child and always wanted lots of children herself but they just had two. She would always welcome our friends and tell us to include everyone. Anyway these two children joined in with our game and mum was batting. Mum was competitive and dad was too, when we played games we were never allowed to win, we had to win fairly and squarely. Games were always aimed at our ages and ability so that we absolutely could win if we played well. Mum was Batting well and had picked up about 10 runs. Dad was bowling, he had played cricket for many years at a good local level and was a spin bowler and wicket keeper. Dad bowled to her and she took a swing and away went the ball for a six. The little lad who had just joined us with his sister and was clapping and shouted "go on Super-gran". We all fell about laughing. Mum was a bit speechless but was laughing her head off too. She said to him I'm not a gran yet cheeky. His reply but your hairs white Mrs you must be a gran. That made us all laugh even more. Mums hair had always been salt & pepper for many years, gradually getting whiter and whiter. As a child she had black hair and she started acquiring white hairs at about 19 I think. So by the time we got to this point I was about 9 and my sister was about 12 so mums hair was definitely more white than black, so you could definitely understand that little boys thinking. Mum never forgot that little boy and that story has been told many many times and our own boys also called her super gran, which always made her smile.

Mum was gentle and caring as a mum and would always protect us but she was practical. I had shocking eyesight as a child and fell a lot and tripped a lot and sat within inches of the TV and read with books close up to my nose! When mum first noticed my problems with books up to my nose and shuffling constantly forward to the TV she took me to the doctors and said there is something wrong with her eyes. I was about 12 months old at the time and apparently the doctor sent her away and told her she was being an overbearing mother who was worrying way too much and there was absolutely nothing wrong with me. Well mum told dad when she got home that she was having absolutely none of this because he was definitely wrong! So she booked an appointment at the private optician in our local main street and took me there to see them. They confirmed that I had a severe problem with my left eye especially, an ambyopia, but I was long sighted in both eyes. Therefore my mum was absolutely right I did have eye issues. From that point on I wore glasses, like bottle bottoms, as my dad used to say. My eyes were constantly checked by the private optician and she made sure that the doctor who told her she was an over worrying mother was aware that he was wrong.

I still have scarred knees now to prove just how bad my eyes were but mum always picked me up and brushed me down, doused us both in Dettol, when needed, just in case we had any bugs in the scrapes and covered us in an appropriately huge plaster until it was time for "the air to get to it". One such Saturday I had fallen off the monkey bars while in the "rec" with my sister, (Thats a recreation ground to anyone not understanding Yorkshire slang) my sister dragged me home where mum sat me on the worktop to scrub my knees, whilst interrogating my sister as to how this had happened. Multi-tasking at its best! Special forces and MI5 had nothing on my mum for finding out the truth! She gave me a kiss and told me I was fine and no need for the drama of crying so I sat sniffing and snotting a lot instead. My glasses had snapped clean in two, I had cut my knees, my elbows, my hands and face as i'd landed flat on the concrete floor. As mum was cleaning me up dad was temporarily mending my glasses as opticians were not open on a Saturday afternoon and I would be blind until Monday otherwise. Dad melted the central nose piece over the gas ring of the cooker and pressed back together to form a bridge. He had hands of steel did my dad. He was a gas engineer and plumber and worked with his hands so melted plastic was no issue to him. He wanted to check the bridge was the right shape and placed the glasses on my already scuffed nose to check. He didn't realise my nose was a lot softer than his hands as he placed them on my nose I screamed a whole fresh set of wailing due to blisters now on my nose from very warm melted plastic. Dad was shouted at for being ridiculous, I was cuddled again and told to shhhh whilst mum and dad giggled at the whole situation. I think my sister got away with being told off for not bringing me back in one piece as dad was in more trouble. I had a warm Dettol bath, which does kill every known germ dead but my goodness does it sting! Clean Pyjamas after the bath were compulsory but I did get two chocolate digestives for supper as I had, had a bad day. She adored us and loved us but there was no amateur dramatics or over indulgence or hysteria tolerated.

We were always brought up to tell the truth and mum always said regardless of what it was she would be there for us. If we had committed wrong doing she would take us to the police herself if necessary but we had to tell her the truth so she could help us and support us. In return she always told us the truth in a way we could understand for our age. Anyway, I remember when The Yorkshire Ripper was terrifying the Yorkshire region and every news headline at the time had some detail or another. Grandma and Grandad were at our house (you remember the religious ones) and I was laid in front of the fire either colouring or reading and mum and grandma and grandad

were watching the 6 o'clock news.
For those of younger years, we only had 3 channels to choose from and it was always what your parents wanted to watch and you were the remote control so I wasn't taking much notice of the boring news as I saw it. Anyway I remember the headlines reporting the death of another lady and The Yorkshire Ripper was believed to be responsible. The background of the lady was given out and it was believed that she was an "innocent victim not a prostitute". The language of the press and police left a lot to be desired at the time but that's another story. Anyway I was probably about 8 years old at the time and as children do, I asked what a prostitute was. I wanted to know what other women victims had done that made them not "innocent". Mum answered that a prostitute was a lady who was paid money by men to kiss them and to do things that people who were married did and they generally did it because they had a very bad life and needed to do this for the money not because they wanted to. My

response apparently was "Ok, that's sad". Mum said yes indeed it is. Go and get yourself bathed and ready for bed. I thought nothing more of it but apparently mum had got into trouble from her parents for telling me what a prostitute was but mum and dad would never lie to us when we had asked a question, that is what they believed. They adjusted it so that what they told us was age appropriate but they never lied or avoided telling us things. It makes me proud that they did this as we as children were always aware of other people's circumstances and that not everyone in life was as fortunate as we were. This is something I've done with my own child.

Mum was an amazing champion of anyone she cared for. She would never see advantage taken of them especially my dad or us. I remember an occasion when a local shop owner hadn't paid his somewhat large bill for over three months. Dad who was now running his own business, and had been for some years, had rung and politely reminded him on a couple of occasions and nothing had materialised. Mum went into the shop on a Saturday morning, if my memory serves me correctly, and ordered enough provisions to feed a small army and I could see the shopkeeper almost rubbing his hands in glee at the bill mum was ringing up in his very busy shop. Mum placed all the groceries into her shopping bags, as you did then, as he said the price, Mum looked up and said loudly enough for the busy shop to hear but not loudly enough to shout "I'll pay your bill when you put your hand in your pocket and pay my husband for the work you owe him for and that he's been waiting 3 months for". At that point my eyes very nearly popped out on cartoon like stalks as I knew some kind of point was being made but as I was only about seven or eight I wasn't sure what kind of point. With that my mum took my hand and said "come on love" and off we went home. Surprisingly by the following Monday lunchtime the bill owing was paid in full. Mum did not suffer fools gladly or people hurting those she cared for.

As a Grandma mum was even more ferocious and would even stand against me and my sister as mums, to give "her boys" all the love she could. One day I had come home from work early with the beginnings of a migraine. My thoughts were to collect Jack, my son, from Grandma and Grandads and go home. I usually collected him at about 6pm after finishing work at 5 but it was much earlier at about 4.30 this particular day. I walked in and mum was, as usual, in the kitchen, but minus her usual smile to greet me. She looked at me her face not impressed and said "what are you doing here?". No query as to why I was early or if I was ok at all. I said I had a migraine starting and needed to get jack so I could take my medication and go to bed at the same time as Jack and then hopefully wake the next morning minus the bad head. "Well you can't have him, he's eating tea." "No worries I'll have a cuppa" I said thinking 'ooooh ok, someone isn't happy', trying to work out if it was me, dad or Jack in trouble. I went to the dining room expecting to see Jack eating.

We were always brought up to eat at the table and no exception to this rule and I assumed he would be here too. No one was there so I looked at mum and she huffily but sternly said "he's in the living room watching Scooby!". I walked into the living room and there indeed he was, in his grandma's seat, remote control in hand watching TV. Open mouthed I looked at mum who was bustling in behind me, with a tray of food, like Mrs Overall. She looked me directly in the eye and firmly said "I don't care he needs to relax after school and not have more rules!". Open eyed I looked from one to the other and Jack said very huffily "Mummy I'm not coming home It's Grandma's day! As a five year old he was very vocal in his love of his Grandma and Grandad and I was firmly put in my place. This made me chuckle and as I walked away mum was clucking around Jack, putting a towel over his legs, as he had his shorts on, so the tray wasn't cold on them and giving him his tea. I went to make a cuppa and mum came back into the kitchen preparing Jack's pudding of Strawberries and cream. She was grumbling she, had had to walk up the street three times to get the fruit today. I asked why she bothered and he could have had other fruit. Her response as always was because they are his favourite....and he's my grandson and I'll do what I like. Me firmly put back in my place.....again. Regardless of this she always still expected manners and no being rude from them always. Old fashioned values. She absolutely adored her boys and would always put them first, even in front of her girls if she needed to. But she absolutely loved her family always.

Mum always stood up for herself too although she was not one to cause a stir she would stand her ground. Dad played local cricket every weekend and mum helped make cricket tea's, as was the thing in the 70's and all the kids played in the fields surrounding the ground. Only coming back for tea to eat what the players had left. Some of the younger ladies one day, mum included, one wonderful British summer when it had been particularly damp and cold suggested it maybe an idea for the players if they served soup and bread as an option as well as sandwiches to keep them warm. Well apparently they may as well of suggested an orgy at tea for the uproar it caused on the Ladies "Tea's" Committee. But mum and her friends stuck to their guns, initially just bringing soup for their own husbands and then bringing flasks as others also asked for soup. Resignations were threatened by the older ladies but eventually all was sorted but mum was not one to be pushed around by anyone.

As I've already said mum had a tough childhood from 13 years old when she had to care for her mum who was a semi-invalid and also her grandma who was bed ridden and an invalid too. She wanted us to be prepared for life no matter what it threw at us, as she always said that life will always test you. So we always did little jobs around the house baking and cooking when we were younger when we stood on chairs to mix buns and Yorkshire Pudding batter. Polishing silver and brasses at the kitchen worktop whilst mum cleaned up. Dusting skirting boards, folding clothes, handing ironing to her, cupboard cleaning. All little jobs and they increased as we got older to such things as cutting the grass and ironing so that we could run a house, drive a car and do the basics like changing a tyre, replace oil. But i'm so pleased that between mum and dad they did this as we were fully prepared for coping with life and all it's rollercoaster of up's and down's. And believe me life has thrown many curve balls my way but mums words ring in my head regularly when taking deep breaths and adjusting to cope with different levels of stress.

I suppose our younger days were very un-PC as far as child rearing goes these days but we were brought up to be polite and use manners as they were important in life, to be clean, tidy and respectful to others and always help others when we could. Mum and dad made sure we were always prepared for every eventuality in life. We could cook, clean, wash, iron and drive, change a car tyre, spark plugs and windscreen wipers, as well as bake, decorate and sew clothes. Mum never ever wanted us to go through what she had at 13 and be unprepared for life's curveballs. Dad was also a man before his time he would change nappies, bath us, feed us, read us bedtime stories, take us to ballet and gym class to give mum a break. They worked so well together and we only appreciate how well they worked together now as adults and can see how much they became broken as a pair and lost as their illnesses overtook them and they were no longer able to be that amazingly strong unit that they were as a couple.

5. Changes

The changes that come with dementia do not come in a barrage that widen your eyes or as an assault that slaps your face but more in a drip that passes you by in an almost invisible way until they become so large that they are actually so obvious you question how you have missed them in the first place.

You then realise that you are in fact possibly running another house as well as your own and you haven't even noticed. This leaves you totally wide eyed and questioning your own sanity and thinking that it's actually a problem with you. One of the first instances that made me wide eyed was mum not knowing who I meant when I mentioned my other half and his daughter on fathers day in June in about 2016. I mentioned his name and mum was completely blank as to who he was and questioned me as if I was having a illicit affair. I repeated twice that Andy was who I lived with and Lottie was his daughter but her eyes were blank. I was lost and had run out of explanation options as I'd lived with Andy for about 7 or 8 years at this point. Suddenly she said "oh yes of course", she then looked at me with a look that laid full blame at my feet and said "well you've lived with so many it's hard to keep up!" My sister who was sat in the other chair absolutely fell about laughing, as you do in families, as my jaw hit the floor. "Bloody Hell Mum!" I shrieked! "yes 50% more than you but I've still only lived with two men!!" Absolute shrieks of laughter from my sister continued as I got up and made a drink of tea.

My sister followed me into the kitchen and I looked at her somewhat concerned and asked if she thought something was wrong. She laughed again and said "what just cos she called you a tart?". I did say it wasn't just that and mentioned a few other odd things. She was certain it was the stress of looking after dad who had advance COPD that made her memory wobble at times but we decided to keep an eye on it. This was in the June of 2016 I think.

By the Christmas of the same year Mum rang me in an absolute distraught state on 22nd of December sobbing uncontrollably as she had a piece of ham from the butchers and didn't know what to do with it. By the time I actually got her calm enough to explain in a way I could understand I realised she hadn't just forgotten and ingredient or forgotten the temperature she really didn't know what to do with the piece of ham at all. There was a whole piece of information missing.

I jumped in the car and drove the few minutes to mum and dads and mum was snotty and red eyed and totally irate with confusion. I said come on it doesn't matter lets do it together. We salted the ham and put in the roasting tin, as mum had taught me and how my grandma had taught my mum before me. She sobbed quietly while we did it. I put the dish in the oven and turned it on for roasting. Dad was looking at me absolutely panic stricken saying everything was fine but mum was just too busy and we needed to help more and mum kept saying she was fine now she just got confused with everything she had to do. I made a cup of tea and sat and had a natter for half an hour, I told her when to take the ham out and told dad too and went back home. As soon as I got in I rang my sister and explained. There was silence on the phone and then she said "mmmm, I think your are right there's a problem isn't there".

As I told her it wasn't just that she could not remember the spices we salted the ham with or the oven temperature it was the whole process that had fallen from her head, so yes there absolutely was a problem but I wasn't sure seeing how badly mum and dad reacted that we would actually get anywhere trying to sort out the subject but we would have to try.

That same Christmas mum lost the Christmas cards that I had sent her and dad and that Jack had sent his Grandma and Grandad. I had given her them in early December when I gave out my family cards, one from me and my other half and one from my son to his Grandma and Grandad. She had put them away safe and then couldn't find them to put them on the mantle shelf. Mum called me and again was utterly hysterical and distraught. Dad asked me to go and buy more so that the gap on the mantle piece was filled but mum was absolutely against that and hysterically so. She wanted the ones I had sent her and no others would do. So I had to come home from work early and spent a good couple of hours looking for the cards. All the time I was there mum was pacing and sobbing, shaking and endlessly smoking because she knew she was struggling and her stress levels were through the roof. Eventually and thankfully I found the original cards in the spare bedroom within a pile of books that had been tidied up. They were slotted in between. Something anyone would do but the reaction was so over the top and beyond a reasonable response it worried me deeply. Mum wasn't even able to put together the steps needed to find things misplaced. That is something everyone does at every stage of life.

I spoke to a friend who's mum had dementia and went through some of the things that were worrying me and she agreed that the things I had said were worrying and did seem to point towards memory problems and that the best way forward would be to get mum to the GP if possible but that can be easier said than done. She also gave me an analogy of what happens to the sufferers emotions when they suffer with memory problems caused by Dementia. She likened the functions and emotions in the brain to being two separate book shelves, one for each. The "functional" shelf has no way of holding the books in place if the shelf is rocked and so shaking the shelf will randomly knock off "functions". The "emotions" shelf has tight bands holding the emotions books on the shelf and glass doors across the front. This means even when someone shakes them they do not drop off. So what happens in short is that functions randomly fall off the shelf and they are lost from the memory but the emotions stay put and do not fall. The problem is this means that the emotional response is very heightened in comparison to functions. So anyone suffering any kind of memory loss will be extremely upset and dismissing this upset will escalate the emotions so we need to deal with it by responding differently and helping that person to calm down but using distractions rather than rational reasoning. This confirmed my worst fears really but it made no difference really as I knew we would have a battle on our hands to get mum to go to a doctors.

Mums handbag became a lethal weapon overtime as she was still shopping at this time and but she couldn't manage change so always gave notes in payments but threw the change into the bottom of her handbag. Mum had never done this she had always been in full control of all the household money. She knew where every penny was and went and everything was fully accounted for. As we stood at this point every month we had to go though her handbag and bag up the loose change and change it back into notes. Every month we would change about £30 plus worth of change that was drifting around in the bottom of her handbag. That handbag would have taken out Tyson Fury if she had swung it. But also she had much less knowledge about what was going on money wise in the house. She would regularly ask us to buy things because she had forgotten things when shopping but this became a daily phone call to both me and my sister and we could almost have rented a room in Tesco's we were there so often.

I was looking for some wrapping paper because mum was too tired to be bothered looking one day and she didn't know where it was. Now mum had always put the paper in a specific place. I looked there and it was not there so I thought i'd look in the wardrobe where the Christmas bag was. On looking in here I saw a rolled up plastic bag full of my mums blood pressure tablets and aspirin tablets. There were about half a dozen boxes of medication squirrelled in the back of the wardrobe. I could almost hear the bells literally clanging in my head so I began to go through other drawers and cupboards. In total I found 18 boxes of medication going back over about two to three years squirrelled in different places in drawers and cupboards upstairs.

Most importantly I found what mum wanted and took it down to her with my lets just pretend everything is normal face on but I wrapped up the medication and took it home and rang my sister straight away. We decided to ask dad if mum was taking her blood pressure medication and go from there. Getting dad on his own for long enough was a problem but eventually I asked dad and he said "why would I know it's not my medicine!" About as much help as a poke in the eye so I asked mum if she was still taking her medicine. Arsey does not cover her response to me but I was transported back to being about 10 years old and questioning my mums authority. I definitely had anxiety and was feeling very stressed at this point but I had to keep going. Eventually she said no she wasn't and had no intention to as she couldn't be bothered faffing on a morning with all that and anyway she hadn't taken it for weeks and she was fine so she obviously didn't need it! And that is that, was the response. I was in no uncertainty that, that was the end of the conversation and I was not going to get any further with the conversation.

I rang the GP and asked for a chat for myself and my sister about mum. This was the hardest thing to do but had to be done. To cut a long story short our family GP told us that mum hadn't refilled her prescription for 12 months and when I showed him the bag of medication we all realised there was a problem but the most important thing was to get mum back on her medication. Easier said than done. This was taken out of our hands totally as mum passed out in the street and was brought home by a car driver who witnessed the collapse.

Dad rung me in full panic saying I needed to go up because mum had fallen and cut herself and Louise was cleaning her up but wanted me to check her out as I was first aid trained. Off I went full speed up to their house. I looked at my sister and could see the expression on her face there was something more to this. Mum had a couple of what would be beautiful black eyes, the top of her feet were grazed and cut open along with her knees along with top of her hands. Her palms were cut free so she had not put her hands out at all and had absolutely face planted the floor. The driver of the car who saw her had said that is exactly what it looked like but mum venomously denied it and said she just tripped and refused the GP and was irate at the mention of an ambulance to check her.

Anyway I checked her over and nothing was broken but insisted on a doctor to come out and rang the surgery just in time before closure and the GP came. This gave us the opportunity to mention the lack of medication taken. The only thing that the GP could find was that mum's blood pressure was very high. No shock there then as she face planted the floor and hadn't taken her blood pressure medication for over 12 months! Anyway she agreed to return to taking the tablets as there was a need for them and the doctor booked her an appointment for the following week just to check her out when things had settled he said but taking into account the conversation we had had about her memory. That conversation absolutely sticks in my mind like glue to this day and I can see my mums seething expression when the Doctor talked about her memory due to her stopping taking the blood pressure tablets. Mum was absolutely having none of it and was furiously simmering looking at the doctor like death! She told him in no uncertain terms that it was her decision to stop taking the tablets and there was nothing wrong with her mind so he could stick his tests.

I have to say I took my hat off to him, he persuaded her just to have the basic ten question test and we supported what he said, which did not go down well, and was accompanied with a "wait til I get you out of here!" stare. Out of the 10 questions he asked mum only got 3 right. I was willing her to prove us wrong but my worst thoughts came true. The doctor told her she should have a scan and further memory tests and she told him, in no uncertain terms, absolutely no way! She didn't need to be subjected to ridiculous questions to know there was nothing wrong with her and she was not going anywhere for tests for people to try and prove she was losing her marbles! With that she cut him off mid sentence and left, leaving us behind. He said to us to keep a check and notes of significant things if we could and that we may never get her to have a formal diagnosis so we may not get an access point to formal help. This was the biggest hinderance we would struggle with. After this mum was very very prickly with us both for a couple of weeks but eventually she came round, bless her.

Throughout this time what myself and my sister didn't realise was that we ourselves had been doing more and more house work, shopping, cleaning, ironing, gardening etc and didn't even particularly realise it. We were like R2D2 and C3PO. One of us would call every night and we would put washing in, peg out washing to dry or put it in the dryer, iron, hoover, run round with a duster, put the bins out, clean the fridge, defrost the freezer, order the shopping on line, clean out the fridge, cook which eventually turned into meals on wheels, garden, decorate etc etc. Unfortunately due to dad's own medical conditions he was unable to do the majority of these jobs but he also could not cope at all with the thought of mum being ill. Mum being ill shook his very foundations so if my sister and I carried on doing everything he could maintain his ostrich position and pretend nothing was wrong as everything would carry on the same as usual.

Regularly I would have a call from mum in a state of distress or from dad, with mum hugely distressed in the background because she couldn't eat because she couldn't find her teeth. She would take them out and squirrel them in the most unusual places. She was always so distraught that you couldn't make sense of things so we had to have a cup of tea, calm her down and then almost make a game of hunt the teeth. Looking in any scrunched up tissues in bins pockets of every item of clothes, in amongst socks in the drawers in her bedroom once, she had put some socks away and the teeth had gone with them, in her handbag regularly, in the fridge once and also on top of the butter dish. She had picked the butter dish up to put it away and the teeth went with it. The problem was keeping her calm whilst searching.

The worst thing we had to do and do without mum noticing was to ensure the problems with decaying food in fridges and cupboards didn't lead to either mum or dad becoming ill. We had to check the cupboards and pantry and fridge for food that had gone off or was mouldy or was out of date. When she was still able to shop she would just buy food without checking it was needed and we would find food such as the fresh veg and meat etc all in varying stages of decay. This was why we went down the track of us doing the shopping and then the meals on wheels as all the fresh fruit, veg and meat was going off and rotten but mum was still attempting to cook it and we were petrified they would both end up with with food poisoning or botulism or both. I once went into the garage fridge for some veg, as she asked me to as she couldn't find it and we were hunting onions, and found what I thought was a dead cat going by the smell and the amount of fur as I opened the fridge door. I slammed the door shut in horror but the smell brought my stomach contents up onto the garage floor. On closer inspection it was a brown paper bag full of sprouts that must have been in the fridge with other veg since Christmas and she had forgotten they were there. It was, if memory serves me right April at this point. Dad didn't know they were there and couldn't really get to the garage to look so until I opened the door no one had noticed. Every time we called both me and my sister would make a cup of tea under the pretence of making everyone a drink, whilst scurrying around checking for mould on anything and quickly throwing it in the outside bin. Mum caught my sister once and she was furious as we were checking up on her and thought she couldn't look after them, when she was the one who had taught us how to keep a house. Days of not speaking to us again. So in short we had to tread lightly but had to ensure their safety too.

As time went on mum was becoming less able to function at all independently away from home and any amount of stress would send her blood pressure up and she would fall or as we now know it, have a mini stroke. Twice we had people fetch her home as they had witnessed her fall and had picked her up. But the injuries were always to her face and the back of her hands, knees and the top of her feet, so she never ever put her hands out so was not fully conscious when she fell. Gradually she became less able to manage outside the four walls of home and became agitated and unable to cope, so we took on everything that involved outside and communication to prevent her anxiety increasing and causing falls. Dad could manage small trips up to our shopping in main street for little bits from local shops on his mobile scooter but he would also supply her with cigarettes, chocolates and cake much to our despair. We repeatedly told him the dangers of letting her eat these things because of her diabetes and thyroid issues and also smoking wasn't helping in anything at all other than being a crutch to mums agitation but dad's focus was just to make her happy as that would enable his life to remain the same and not change in any way.

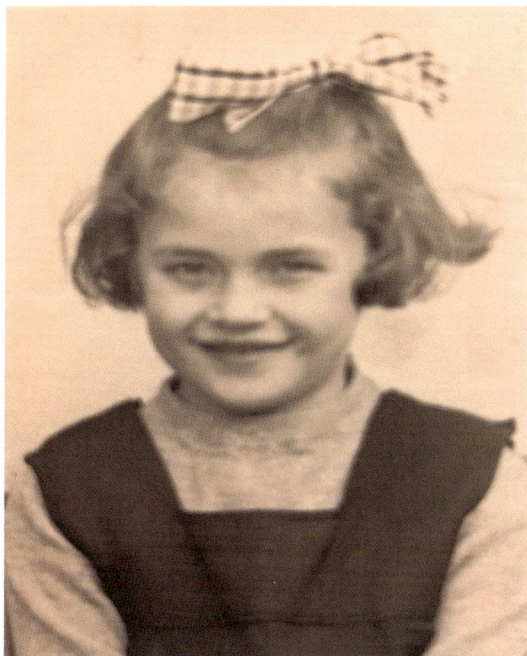

Mum aged about 6 and with her
parents on a family holiday in
Bridlington, East Yorkshire.

Mum front an centre as netball captain
at school and in her hairdressing days
with a different hair colour.

Mum and dad when they first started "courting" and on their wedding day.

Mum with me on my wedding day and with dad on their Golden Wedding anniversary.

My big sister and I, when I was 1 and she was 4, and a few years later when we were older than 1 and 4.

Mum & Dad, grandma & grandad, with their boys Lewis at the top and Jack at the bottom.

6. Talking & Floundering

Although we look back on these tales now and can on occasions laugh fondly at the time we went through them we were literally living on a knife edge for years. Every time my phone rang I was in panic as to what may be the reason for the call. I permanently had my phone attached to me and would never leave it behind or risk not answering it. Our own anxiety levels must have been through the roof, when I look back, and for such a long period. I had never even noticed that I was anxious if I didn't have my phone or if I missed a call until I took a business retreat and friends there who hadn't seen me for a while pointed out the obvious, which was the heights of my anxiety.

We spoke to dad on many occasions individually and both my sister and I together trying to reason with him when anything happened and also when things got on top of us. I will be honest and say this was not always a rational calm discussion because the stress levels were up through the ceiling and we just wanted to make sure they were safe. Dad wanted both him and mum safe but wanted to achieve that with myself and my sister, only, caring for them. He wasn't having anything to do with anyone else being involved. His statement for years was "all we are asking for is a little bit of help from you as our daughters, Is that too much to ask?". The guilt involved in us not being able to care for them as dad wanted was a huge burden, but equally made us both angry, fearful and resentful, at our own lives being stifled, which then in turn makes you feel guilty for being such ungrateful, uncaring daughters. Ultimately you are also fearful that your life is changing because your parents are becoming frail and on the last part of their path in life and no one really wants to see that so brutally shoved in their faces.

Dad eventually admitted that there was an issue in one particularly upsetting discussion we had, that left all three of us in tears but he was absolutely resolute that they only needed us to help more and things would be fine. No amount of us telling him that looking after them and their house as well and their financials, and our own houses, working full time and caring for children was working. His ostrich syndrome had an amazing capacity no matter how obvious mums frailty and confusion became. Following the doctor's short memory consultation he told us that there definitely was a problem but mum had to be totally complicit and understanding in the progression of the tests to come to a final diagnosis of the dementia. Dad and mum refused the need to get any further tests done so unfortunately my sister and I were left with the Hobson's Choice of caring for mum and dad ourselves as much as we possibly could, while falling apart ourselves and with dad ignoring the fact that we were slowly sinking under the stress.

Between us we covered almost every day of the week calling in and doing jobs such as bobbing washing in, pegging it out or drying in the dryer, changing beds, putting bins out, ironing, shopping, cleaning, gardening are the very basics we covered but everything you could think of ended up being what we did. One of us calling in each day and letting the other know what jobs we had done and what needed doing. If we didn't do this mum may occasionally put washing in the dryer and we wouldn't know and it could sit there for days and then end up mouldy as happened on more than one occasion as the food did that was put in dressers or wardrobes or left in car boots. So we had to be very much on the ball all the times. On many occasions dad would ring very upset whilst I was at work or my sister was at work and say we needed to go down because he couldn't get his socks on and mum couldn't manage it for him. He could not longer wash himself and mum couldn't help him so that became another job for us.

I could see my sister was at complete breaking point and I wasn't far behind. Our health and our family life was suffering. We could no longer have days out unless the other was staying at home we struggled to go on holiday's and we most certainly could do nothing together as sisters or as families. We sat one evening and decided we had to speak to dad about cleaners and gardeners to at least take that load from us and we could at least stand a chance of holding everything else up. Dad was having none of it! If we would just help more then they'd be absolutely fine. This was his constant statement as he did not want anyone else involved, he just wanted him and mum safe and life to stay the same. Eventually after some heated discussions we managed to persuade dad to have a cleaner and gardener, who were recommended by people they knew and so felt happy with. Despite dad preferring us to do these things as it was cheaper and apparently easier, we stood our ground and the cleaner and gardener were firmly put into action and deemed ok, if we weren't going to give them a bit of help. The guilt was always drip fed consistently. He had an amazing ability to manipulate and make you feel incredibly guilty for none compliance but we had to stand together or we wouldn't be able to do anything at all to help mum and dad.

When we reached this point we decided to speak to mums doctor to see if there was anything we could do to put help in place and make sure mum and dad were safe but without the formal diagnosis as mum and dad still refused to go to the doctors as nothing was wrong. I'm sure you can hear my eye's rolling from where you are! I spent a lot of time in frustration and rolling my eyes as my anxiety was through the roof on a permanent basis and I was like a cat on a hot tin roof, to coin a phrase, and I know my sister was on a higher level than me. The only help we could get turned out to be a social worker who was appointed as a carer for carer's if you like. So therefore she was there to care for us as carers. She sat and listened a lot and listened a bit more to everything we said and asked a lot of questions about who did what for mum and dad. All I can say is she was a fabulous lady who had an amazing amount of empathy with the right amount of truthfulness and a lot of problem solving abilities. She was very blunt and said if we did not stop doing everything we were doing we would break and be in a worse state than our parents and we needed to get carers in regardless of what mum and dad said to allow them to care and for us to be daughters again as we were not being daughters at all, in any way anymore, we were carers. It was the only way we could make them, or mainly dad, acknowledge the problem if we took away us doing everything and therefore he would acknowledge the fact we did everything and made it brutally obvious to dad that help had to be given from the channels that were built to give help.

To demonstrate how over stretched we were she held up two lists of answers to questions she had asked us. These were different jobs and who did them. One piece of paper had general weekly cleaning and grass cutting written on the A4 sheet. On the other list, every other household job known to mankind was written on it and that was the list my sister and I did. This A4 sheet was full completely. It was definitely a very visual picture of how stretched we were. It also made us realise how much we were putting stress on our own families as they were picking up things in our own homes so we could do everything at mum n dads.

We knew we had to do this and she was right, once we saw the evidence written in a list in front of us but getting Dad to agree was a whole different ball game. Dad was a typical

Yorkshire man, he had an opinion and was not really up for moving from it regardless. He wanted his plan playing out how he wanted it playing out regardless of what problems it caused to others. Anyway we hatched a plan, mum was struggling to shower herself any longer and my closest friend was a carer within the community and mum and dad had known her for years as she was a hairdresser and did their hair. She had kept mum and dad on when she had changed career paths. She knew how things were because she was my friend and had said from the beginning she would help if she could, but mum and dad had always refused. However a little plotting and seed planting from Julie while she washed mums hair one day led to the opportunity of Julie saying "well why don't you get a shower while I'm here and that will mean you don't have to do it when the girls come home from work and you are so tired by that time". Mum and dad thought it was their idea that Julie would just come and help mum shower as we could do everything else and didn't need her, but the main thing was the foundations had been laid.

Before long my wonderful friend was showering both mum and dad, making sandwiches, checking they had had their tablets when they should have tablets and calling in at tea time to put their meals on wheels out for them twice a week. She managed to persuade them to do that one on her own without a word from us. It was like watching magic happen. We slowly felt the weight not leaving us but at least lifting for 2 days a week when she would see to them and just text us to let us know how they were. Two days where we didn't have to go from work and could eat tea before ten at night. Sounds ridiculous but that was absolutely amazing and it meant we could actually go to bed and sleep on those nights as we could ring them but would not have to go to the pressure cooker of fear, confusion, needs and demands, where our forever growing job list was continually added to.

We plodded along like this for a while with my friend Julie seeing them two days a week and she was amazing with mum and dad, although dad moaned incessantly about the cost of a cleaner and a gardener when we could do things for free and the meals on wheels two days a week when it would be easier if we cooked, our response was "easier for who dad?", and he would stop for a day or two. He also thought Julie was amazing, which was a huge blessing! Told us regularly how glad he was that he'd asked her to start helping out. This point usually involved a huge eye roll from me and a sarcastic "I bet you are!". Dealing with dementia gives you and amazing ability to cope with difficult and stressful situations but also gives you a dark sense of humour and a slightly unhealthy love of sarcasm. To be fair I think we were always sarcastic so it just enhanced it. The best part about Julie being there was she knew our thought direction was to get mum diagnosed so that we could access as much help as we could for her and for mum & dad as a couple. Carer's are totally undervalued in my opinion. The ones who stay at this job really are not doing a job they are following a calling to a vocation and absolutely should be paid at least 4 times what carer's are paid at the moment, especially by care homes!

The initial point of the GP noting a memory issue was followed by a horrendous follow up with a specialist dementia nurse where mum walked out of the appointment and gave my sister and I a verbal roasting about thinking she's was mad and daring to treat her like an idiot. She swore blind she knew nothing about the appointment or having seen the GP six weeks before. It was one of the most distressing events we went through for all of us and we knew we would end up having to do this again at some point to get a diagnosis and help so we had to plough on regardless, slowly pushing forward. Keeping dropping hints, mentioning, explaining, suggesting. Getting shot down in flames every time and also knowing we would get shot down but at every point where mum would fall, forget things and people, get lost up the street, lose her teeth, loose her purse, leave the gas cooker on and all the other little minor things in between we kept working towards this goal and Julie also kept working with us. On top of all this dad could be aggressive and abusive if he didn't get his own way about us being there all the time to care for them. This came from fear and frustration as well as his own illness, but still cuts deep. He was scared about what would happen to them both because of his failing health and mums. He didn't want to leave where they were. He just wanted his family around him and be safe and life not to change. Unfortunately this approach was making things worse in the way we were able to care for them as the lack of acknowledgement just made the situation unmanageable and acutely painful for everyone. But we had to keep trying and keep asking to get what, above all, mum needed. Eventually she agreed to go and speak to the GP again and because of the narrative of events we were able to give the GP and with mums agreement we were able to go for a brain scan.

7. Life lost and taken over

It was a beautiful sunny day when we went to see mum's favourite doctor for her results. He was the only one who knew what he was doing apparently. To mum the sun literally shone down Dr Richolds trouser legs she had so much faith in him. Me and my sister, with mum tottering between us, suddenly she looked very little and quite frail. We went through the diagnosis with the doctor and it was all my worst fears confirmed. Vascular Dementia with scaring from previous stokes already and too advanced he believed, from the results, for medication to help in any way but he would refer us to the dementia specialist and to social services to have access to help. This was a very hollow victory I can honestly say. As we walked out of the doctor's surgery I can honestly say I felt physically sick and my head was spinning, tears ran down my face behind my sunglasses. Mum chatted normally as we drove back home saying "You see I don't need any tablets!". All I could think was that we had a death sentence and I was going to lose my mum a lot sooner than I would of ever envisaged. My sister and I looked at each other sideways as we drove home listening to mum and joining in with her thoughts about how lovely Dr Richold was and how he wouldn't give you tablets when they weren't necessary and a lot of doctors could learn from that. The expected life time line for vascular dementia is between 3 to 5 years from onset. We of course were not aware of the exact date of onset so had no idea how far along this line we were. The following day we had a call from the social services contact we had made months previously ourselves to help establish help for mum and dad and a call from the dementia specialist to book an appointment to come out and see mum. The ball was certainly rolling. Faster than dad was happy about as he didn't want people involved but now had no option with the worst case scenario diagnosis and probably a lot faster than we expected but getting mum safe and helped in the right way was imperative.

On 6th June in the evening dad rang me to say mum wasn't feeling well so I called up to see them. Mum said she didn't feel ill but she felt funny and her right arm was tingling. She had dropped her overflowing ashtray on the floor and was struggling to grip. I wasn't happy and wanted to ring an ambulance as I was concerned about more TIA's. Dad was absolutely furious with me and refused point blank saying she had a trapped nerve in her neck and there was absolutely no need for all the hoo-ha I was causing. No amount of me explaining the implications changed his opinion and mum was in floods of tears at this point and so agitated because dad was shouting and saying the doctors would take her away that she also refused to let me ring the doctors and said she would ring them in the morning and go to the surgery. My sister walked in half way through this and I explained in the kitchen as she was making mum a drink to try and calm her that my concerns were she was having another TIA. She talked to mum and dad as they had calmed a little and tried to explain again, and once again the balloon went up with dads temper and he was not allowing anyone to take mum anywhere as she didn't want to go anywhere and was fine. So at this point I had to say fine, you leave things as they are but it is on your head dad, I want her to be checked out but if you don't and she doesn't it's your decision. The following morning at 8.45 I got a phone call from dad, mum had fallen on the floor and couldn't get up. I had to throw my poor client out of my clinic and I ran down the road to mum and dads house. I ran through the door or I should say that is what a I attempted to do but nearly broke my arm and face as I hit a locked door! I rang dad and he answered and I pointed out I couldn't get in. His answer was he couldn't get his breath and couldn't open the door so I'd have to get in another way. I told him that would have to be a brick as the key was in the other side of the door and I couldn't get my key in. His response was "well you'll have to then!". So through the window went a brick and my arm through the hole in the glass to turn the key from the inside. I had rung my sister as I ran down the street but she was at the other side of Leeds so would be at least 30 minutes, and as I ran upstairs I could hear mum crying. Dad was sat in his stairlift telling me he needed me to get him to the living room and make a cup of tea. I can't write what I said exactly but needless to say it was roughly that mum was the priority and he would have to get himself down on his stairlift! Mum was facedown between the wardrobe and the bed but fully conscious and crying and I couldn't really get to her. Being first aid trained I checked her for breaks and knew I needed help to get her turned over. I rang Julie and she didn't answer so I had to ring my other half as he worked locally. Dad was shouting not to ring the ambulance but I ignored him this time as I dialled 999. mums knees and elbows were raw and bleeding and I asked her how long she had been on the floor. She replied that it was when she got up to the loo her leg wouldn't work and she fell. Ok but was that first thing just before dad rung me, no she said it was still dark, I've been here ages and I just want to get up cos I'm wet and you're not helping! I could consider myself told. Andy, my other half arrived and we managed to turn her and sat her head and back supported on the bed, no breaks anywhere but scuffed and bleeding knees and elbows. Mum was so upset she was wet but it wasn't just wet she was absolutely soaked. At this point I thought there was something odd about the length of time mum had been on the floor. She was worried at Andy seeing her in her nightie and pants but I told her it was fine he didn't have his glasses on so couldn't see a thing. The ambulance arrived at the same time as my sister did and they began their assessment of mum. I went to dad at this point to clarify the time she fell. It turned out that she had had a full TIA at approximately 4.30 am but dad didn't ring at that time he rang at 8.45am because he said he couldn't get to the phone at mum's side of the bed and couldn't get his breath, due to the severe COPD, so he "encouraged" mum to get up herself but she wouldn't so he had struggled to the phone and managed to ring me in the end. I cannot explain how cross, angry, devastated and upset I was at this point because if we had rung an ambulance the night before as I had told him all this would have been avoided. I had to walk away from him and get in the ambulance with mum. I went to the hospital and my sister stayed with dad and sorted the window out that my carefully aimed brick had gone through.

We had a wonderful trip to hospital and the ambulance crew were amazing with mum as she was so confused and adamant she was getting up and going home because she had nothing wrong with her that a cup of tea and some toast wouldn't solve bless her. We arrived at the hospital and mum was a priority case and was pushed through to have a CT scan as she hit the A & E waiting area. After this we were put in a cubicle and the nurse did her observations. Part of this was taking bloods. She attempted twice, bless her, and looked completely confused as she was unable to extract any blood. She went to get the matron and sure enough she couldn't get any blood either at which point she brought mum the biggest aspirin I have ever seen. It was like the top of a tomatoe sauce bottle. She asked for a word and told me mums blood was so thick it could not be drawn off and was hoping the aspirin would thin her blood before she had any more strokes and they would also be able to get blood for testing but in the mean time could I try and get her to drink water. Yes absolutely was my reply knowing it would be similar to climbing Mount Everest as mum liked tea. Thank goodness for technology as I could text my sister whilst sat with mum persuading her that water was much better than tea. She had no intention of believing me but she sipped at the water, pulling faces at me with every sip, until the bottle was empty. Nurses returned about an hour later and managed to finally get blood.The consistency was still that of warm treacle but at least they got some and her blood was thinning and reducing the chance of a following huge stroke. It was quickly diagnosed as a moderate TIA or stroke in layman's terms and she was admitted, much to her fury, and taken to the stroke ward for aftercare.

My sister arrived at the hospital and we went through all the form filling that was needed and also spoke privately to the nursing staff to update them on how mum was generally and her confusion and dementia. Mum was still very poorly at this point and quiet but still not happy at being in the hospital. The other thing they needed to do was give her the highest dose nicotine patch they could find as she was incredibly aggressive due to the nicotine withdrawal but stopping her smoking at this point I'm sure contributed to her survival.

I must say here in black and white that we are very blessed in the UK because the NHS are the best care facility there is. The nursing staff and doctors are out of this world despite huge pressure and even less finances. The genuine care and love and professionalism they have for their patients and their jobs is second to none.

The second day mum was in hospital she was totally delirious as she had a severe water infection and had no idea where she was, she was suffering hallucinations and was very frightened and aggressive but was still trying persistently to get out of bed to come home. She had 24 hour supervision next to the nurse to make sure she didn't get out of bed as her right arm and leg were no longer working due to the stroke. We spent the next 8 days as a family visiting mum at the hospital while she worked with the nursing and physio teams to help get movement back to her arm and leg. She worked hard, was incredibly focused and fought like a tiger to come home. After ten days they said she could come home and would need to be monitored at outpatients, keep up the exercises and no longer smoking was a must. Her dementia had taken a big drop downwards due to the stroke and she became more confused when out of her normal environment and circumstances. The type of dementia she had, Vascular Dementia, went down in large steps as the disease progresses. Every event that caused deterioration, which ranged from an incident that caused shock to another TIA to a water infection, meant a big change in behaviour rather than a gradual decline that is attributed to other types of Dementia and Altzheimers.

In the time mum was in hospital, the occupational therapists had fitted handrails at home at the door, the toilet and the bathroom. Placed a handrail at the side of her bed, brought a walking frame, adapted the shower for her and made the home more adapted to her. We had also made sure Julie could come in every day, twice a day, sorted meals on wheels every day, and tried to help dad understand the effect the dementia and the stroke would have on mum. Tried to explain he couldn't have her running about doing things for him constantly and couldn't carry trays or two cups of tea because she had no strength to her right side but I knew it wasn't going in. He just wanted her home and them to be together and safe with us caring for them, and their life unaffected.

As each week passed mum would have at least one falling incident each week that would land us in hospital again for a brain scan and it was always involving doing something for dad. Fetching dinner in on a tray, bringing in cups of tea, getting his medication, getting out his mobility scooter from the garage. No amount of us telling him he had to do these things for himself changed things and no amount of us getting in help or being there ourselves helping and doing things was enough to cover every minute of the day to care for them and this was what they needed ultimately. Eventually me and my sister got together with Julie and discussed how to move forward and decided to try the bedroom furniture in the dinning room to bring them down to one level but Julie did say that their care was exceeding her as mum needed two peoples support on some occasions and this would increase as her condition became worse. So basically we would need to look at increased care options. Julie left to go up to mum and dads to do their tea and called me almost immediately to tell me dad wasn't well and she was calling an ambulance.

We followed her up and the ambulance arrived again. Julie sat with mum in the other room and the paramedics worked on dad who was vomiting and couldn't breathe. Again off we went to the hospital. Julie stayed with mum and both me and my sister went to hospital. Dad had had a heart attack and was not expected to live.

My sister had just had Carpel Tunnel surgery so I had to move in with mum as she couldn't be left alone she was far too distressed and her dementia spiralled out of her control and our understanding. Dad was in a coma and the discussion with the specialist was that there was no expectation of him living as he was not responding to any medication. Mum was sundowning, which basically means she was agitated, irritable, restless and unbelievably confused, constantly looking for dad. It was incredibly difficult to get her to settle and to sleep for longer than an hour and she wouldn't stay in bed. She would try to get out of bed but would fall because of her stroke as it had taken the use of her right arm and leg. I was struggling seriously to pick her up off the floor and get her up on my own so my son had to come and stay with me and unfortunately see his grandma in ways no 17 year old should. But he made me so proud of the man he is becoming. He was so patient, caring and loving with her. He would sit and hold her hand and chat about all sorts of inane subjects and make her giggle, but would also reassure her whenever she became anxious. My nephew who had just turned 20 at the time would also come up and spend time with her so that my sister and I could do the practical things that have to continue like food shopping, washing, ironing, cleaning etc and he too was amazing with how he was with her. They are two young men that were challenged and certainly stood up and were counted and made me and my sister so so proud in who they are as people and the young men they are.

I was quickly going down hill, health wise because of my lack of sleep during the night with mum and still trying to work to an extent because I was self employed and couldn't not work. Both me and my sister were sharing the care as much as she could with one arm, and visiting dad everyday too but we were both exhausted and we had to take the decision to put mum into respite care because we were struggling to cope and seriously struggling. The respite care was at Oulton, a small village a few minutes away, who were able to accommodate her dementia. We had looked at quite a few, unfortunately all private, and many didn't unfortunately accommodate dementia, as all the local council run homes had closed due to lack of government funding. The government doesn't recognise Dementia as a terminal illness despite it being that, they consider it a mental health problem, which means it gets very minimal funding care wise in relation to other illnesses and also means relatives have to pay full costs. Mum was not happy in any way at all in going to this place, which was absolutely amazing, but she did not care at all, bless her. She tried to get out of bed every night so had to have alarm and crash mats around the bed as her legs still didn't work well. She was very grumpy with me and my sister when she remembered that we had taken her there and sat with her back to us, arms folded, very like a five year old mid sulk. But a few chocolates would usually soften her resolve. Dad was in a Coma for 7 days and on day 8 woke up and asked for a cup of tea. It was my turn at the hospital to sit with him and as we, me, Andy my parter, my son and my nephew, walked into the Palliative Care ward he was sat with a cuppa in his hand dunking Chocolate biscuits as if nothing had happened and raising the cuppa in a cheers motion to us! I was nearly in the next bed to him with the shock. Something the hospital had not let us know was that he had seemingly recovered so it was a huge shock as we had been told in no uncertain terms that we were at the end of his road. The kids were both ecstatic to see their grandad looking so amazingly well. I rang my sister on face-time, who was with mum, and passed dad over to chat while I went to find a doctor for a chat. Her face looked very much like I imagine mine did when I first saw him with the shock of seeing him.

Dad spent a further 3 weeks in recovery on the heart unit and we had to have a very hard conversation with him about the fact mum was in respite care due to her dementia. He was not happy and wanted her back home ready for him to go back home. We asked him how he would do that when he was unable to walk unaided due to muscle wastage. He was very angry, upset, frustrated and scared and said we would just have to do more to help. We had to be really frank and tell him despite our will to help as much as we could and him wanting us to help them regardless of all else we couldn't leave our jobs and homes to give 24 hour care and keep them at home. We all shed many many tears on this day and it will always remain imprinted in my mind as one of the saddest days. Dad agreed that the only way forward was for them both to go into care with the view of him hopefully recovering enough and gaining enough strength to go back home and only mum staying in the home on a permanent basis.

We managed to find a care home about 20 minutes away that could look after both of them and they moved in together at the end of September 2019.

8. Covid 19

Well I'm sure I don't need to tell anyone what happened in March 2020. One word and that word is Covid. As a sports massage therapist I closed my business as dictated by the government on 23rd March 2020. This day was also the day we were no longer permitted to visit and see our parents in their care-home. My sister and I were the only two people allowed on widow visits once they were organised but no other people were allowed to visit. Window visits were horrendous. Talking through a window to elderly people, who have hearing issues or health issues that prevent comprehension was beyond ridiculous and cruel. We did get special dispensation in the July of 2020, from the home for mum and dad to see my son before he flew to America to play football on a scholarship. I knew it was incredibly likely he would never see them again. Indeed my dad never saw his grandchildren again in person and my mum only just managed to see them in person before her death. We, among thousands of other families were devastated by the following 2 years in ways that could never have been in your thoughts or nightmares.

The nursing home took a couple of weeks to put into place communication between residents and their families and they initially rang us once a week with mum and dad on a WhatsApp video call so they could physically see us. This wasn't too bad for dad who could recognise us and retain interest in conversations and vaguely understood what on earth was going on and chat but mum unfortunately was utterly scrambled by absolutely everything and really struggled to understand her life and spent a lot of time crying, anxious and confused throughout these calls so we had to keep things quite short. As soon as mum became disjointed and agitated we had to end calls and promise to ring again a little later. Obviously we couldn't as calls were on a rota but mum by this point would have forgotten we had rung and spoken to her unless dad or the carers mentioned that we had so she would be calmer in the moment. Which is all we wanted to be honest.

Dad did have a mobile so could call us at any time he wanted to for a chat but they couldn't see us and mum struggled to know how to put a phone to her ear and actually chat anymore so it never worked too well. In fact one day during such conversation dad had passed the mobile to mum, who had put the phone upside down and back to front to her ear. She couldn't hear me at all and just kept laying the phone in her lap saying no one was there and dad was really getting more and more frustrated shouting at her to put it to her ear properly. I couldn't make myself heard to tell dad to calm down because mum just had forgotten how a telephone was used and needed it to be done for her. The next thing I heard was a yelp and a thud and the line went dead. Now mum was a fabulous bowler at rounders and the captain of the team and she was also Goal Shooter and Captain of the Netball team when at school and as such my only conclusion was that she had launched the phone at dad because shouting irritated her head and she couldn't stand it at all. Her agitation always increased if anyone raised voices. So I had to ring the nursing home and ask to be put through to carers on mum and dads floor. I spoke to the carers and told them what happened and they ran quickly down to the room where mum and dad were and I was indeed correct mum had indeed flung the phone at dad and made perfect contact with the side of his head. Dad obviously was tearful as it would most definitely of hurt and mum was in tears too holding her head as raised voices caused her physical pain. The changes that Dementia bring to the party are unlimited and know no bounds and the pain they bring have no depth. The wonderful carers calmed mum and tended to dads head, which thankfully was only bruised and put dad on the phone. I asked if he was ok and he was tearfully and upset at mum launching her hand sized missile at him. I did remind him that unfortunately mum forgot a lot of things and although he was struggling to accept it working with it would be better than trying to battle against it. Calming mum and distracting would be the only way forward for us all and shouting and tantrumming in defiance was not going to make the situation any better at all. Dad cried down the phone and said they just wanted to come home and be with us doing things and didn't want to be with other people doing things. We went through their need for 24 hour care again and dad ended the conversation abruptly saying if we couldn't be bothered to help then they'd just have to stay where they were. The conversation cut short by dad but left me with the huge weight of guilt and tears running down my face for hours as these stressful conversations always did. Dementia leaves scars on everyone it touches.

Whenever the carers called us for a face-time it was lovely to see them sat holding hands as they used to at home, even if they were both snoozing and napping in their chairs whilst watching TV they would be holding hands. The carers would call from the office to update us on anything we needed to know or answer any questions we had and they would then walk into mum and dads room and they would be there holding hands and mum would gaze at dad in such a wonderful way, it was like they were the only two in the room and they just loved each other beyond anything else. Dementia would never take that away.

Some things wouldn't change with mum or were very slow to change, no matter what damage dementia caused to mums brain. I used these as markers to see where abouts roughly her long term memory was. There were two things in life that mum was particularly scared of and that was dogs and thunder and lightening storms. She had been bitten on the face by a Dalmatian when she was about 8 so was very wary of dogs, she wouldn't of harmed them or see any harm come to them but she would't approach them and definitely would not have owned one under any circumstances. I however, since having my own children, have always had a dog, I adore them and mum tolerated them when she came to our house but would roll her eye's at Jack snuggled on the sofa kissing them when he was little. Anyway, if I called at mums with Jack when we had been out walking we were only allowed as far as the kitchen no matter how much Jack begged. Dogs definitely didn't go in mums house further than the kitchen and over her dead body in the living room or on the sofa. She wouldn't leave them outside in the cold because that was mean but absolutely no further than the kitchen. Anyway, I would say to her occasionally shall I bring Coco (our current dog's name) to see you? Just to see her response and if she remembered Coco or would remember her feelings towards dog's. She would look at me and say who? And I would say the dog mum. I would get a very stern but definite "errr NO!! I don't do dogs further than kitchens!". That absolutely never changed.

The other thing that we always worried about and told the nursing home about when she moved in was the fact that mum was terrified of was thunder and lightening storms. When we were younger she would put all the lights on in the house, shut all the curtains and sit in a corner of the dining room that had no windows near her rocking. She would chain smoke, cry, shake, and drink endless tea and would sometimes make herself sick with the anxiety and stress. We all knew that if a thunder storm happened we all had to get home because mum would be in despair until she knew we were all home safe and also we had no chance of going out if one happened while we were getting ready to go out because we were not allowed in the bath or shower or near a door or window. If a storm happened one of us would ring the home and sure enough she would be rocking and crying, thankfully not smoking any more, but still extremely stressed and agitated and unable to eat. Thankfully they could take her to the day room/kitchen area which had no direct windows and they would play music she enjoyed and distracted her with stories and TV programs. The carers always did their best for her in these circumstances. These two things never left her no matter how far along in the dementia journey she was. Mum would sometimes become upset at living in the nursing home, generally because dad would remind her that they weren't at home, which would unsettle her. She would grab at us when we were there and say she just wanted to go home and then cry. Dad would try these guilt tactics to try and get them home and us to move in and look after them rather than nursing care but he did not comprehend how distraught this made mum or the mental and physical impact it had on her. She would say to us initially I just want to go home to Barley Hill Road.

This was the family home that they left to go into the Nursing Home but within months mum would say I just want to go home to Lidgett Lane. We had left that house when I was 6 years old to move to Barley Hill Road so she had lost quite a few years there. I was 48 at this time so she had lost 42 years in where she lived and where "home" was. After dad died she went further back and wanted to go home to her mum and dad in Hemsworth but would sometimes confuse her mum and dad living at Lidgett Lane so there was still long term memory confusion and distortion.

In the Summer of 2020 we could see mum and dad outside the Nursing Home under a gazebo but with a large table between us and just for 20 minutes. We weren't allowed to hold hands or touch mum n dad in any way. No hugging and definitely no kissing and only two family members were allowed in and it always had to be the same two people, which as the only two children for us was fine but this ridiculous regulation crippled other families as children were unable to see parents, grandchildren couldn't see grandparents and so it went on. Our children were unable to see their grandparents other than by Face-time as we would ring them when we were with mum n dad. This would be ok with mum for a few minutes but would eventually distress mum as she couldn't work out where the boys were. So we always made these short and sweet catch ups for them. Towards the end of the summer in 2020 the visits had progressed and we were allowed into the Nursing Home into a room accessible from outside and mum and dad could be brought into the room from the inside of the nursing home. The room had been decorated by the staff as a "fairy dell" but with a floor to ceiling perspex screen between the front door entrance where we entered and the back door entrance where mum and dad came in. Lots of this was never a good experience as mum found this disorientating. She would not be able to talk and would be staring at the screen rather than being able to communicate with us. She would poke and push the screen trying to work out what it was and sometimes would thump at it with tears rolling down her face because she just didn't understand what was happening. Dad was not great at distraction to calm mum and would end up upset and in tears too because he couldn't calm her. Although these visits were still only 20 minutes long they felt like hours and were incredibly painful. I know my sister drove home every time in tears in the same way that I did too struggling with the darkest guilt. By Christmas we were back in lockdown and were unable to visit and were back to face-times with our parents but dad was visibly failing with his COPD and leaking heart valve. He struggled to breath if we were talking to him and was becoming increasingly yellow. Mum was shrinking further and further within herself because dad couldn't talk to her easily to remind her of things and interact as he had. On the 17th of January we were contacted by the nursing home to say dad was in end of life care and we were allowed to go in individually but if we were there mum would not be allowed to be with dad. We argued with them over this and stated that if we had taken a Covid test before entry and were wearing full PPE exactly as the carers were there was no danger to mum or anyone else. They eventually agreed and allowed mum to be with us in the room but me and my sister could only be with dad individually.

On 19th January I had gone to see dad and mum was brought into me after she had had her breakfast. She looked at me blankly until I pulled my mask down slightly and then realised who I was and she absolutely beamed at me and tears were in here eyes and she was grabbing at my hands to hug me. She looked at dad eventually and asked me who was in the bed. I told her it was dad and she told me it wasn't because dad didn't look like that. I told her dad was very poorly and it was him. She said "well I don't like the look of him!" I said to her "well he's looked like this for the last 55 years and you haven't minded so far" She side eyed me with the look that only mothers have and said "There's no need for your smart mouth, you know what I mean!". That was me told and firmly reminded who my mother was. She looked blinking and confused and then suddenly her voice changed and became stronger pulling her shoulders up and back and she said to me "Is he that kind of poorly?" I took a deep breath and replied saying that unfortunately he was that kind of poorly. She asked me how long he was going to be with us and I told her I didn't know but not long. I told her we would sit with him and just be with him as long as we could and she was happy with that but wanted me to make a cup of tea because we would need a strong cup of tea. That made me smile, she seemed to be back in the room very firmly. She was facing dad in her wheelchair and was leaning forward across dad and I was worried she would fall across him. So I said let me just move you back mum and sort the tubes out under the bed and then I can sit you sideways so you can hold dads hand properly. "OK" mum replies, so I shuffled her wheelchair backwards and I was on hands and knees under the bed pushing oxygen tubes and inflation tubes for his inflated mattress and electric cables out of the way. Suddenly I hear dad groaning, my eyes widen and I think the worst is happening. I scuttle out from under the bed and bang my face on mums wheelchair. She pulled herself forward again. "Mum, what are you doing' I said rubbing my face. "well I want to hold your dads hand and I couldn't reach from there so I pulled myself forward. She had forgotten what I had said in the 30 seconds I'd been under the bed. "Mum I'd just put you there so I could move all these cables and then you can hold dads hand properly". Dads groans rang in my ears again and I looked down and mum had wheeled herself onto dad's oxygen line!! In horror I shoved mum back away from it and she looked at me startled. "Mum your wheels were on dads oxygen!". "Oh dear!" she says to me "well that won't end well will it". To be honest we had not laughed like that for a long time and it certainly changed the atmosphere in the room as we both giggled for a long time. Our family have always had a dark sense of humour but I think it does help at times like this. We sat holding hands and talking about childhood holidays and happy memories on and off until it was time for me and Louise to change places. We lost dad at 3.20pm on 20th January 2021. We were all allowed to be together by the nursing home after dad had passed and as we sat together in mums bedroom we could see mums capacity to be her pre-dementia self, as she had been for two days, was ebbing away completely. We had to leave mum in the nursing home that evening and as visiting wasn't permitted at the time due to Covid restrictions within the home so we didn't see mum in person again for several weeks. Mum was also unable to attend dads funeral because she was too ill and would not of remembered he had gone. There is never any point re-telling someone with dementia that a loved one has gone because they grieve all over again like its the first time and to do that is just cruel. So from then on if mum asked where he was he had just popped to the shops and would be back soon.

On the day of dads funeral the carers sat with her most of the day and at the time of the service she shouted out his name and began to cry quietly. Make of that what you will but I know my dad was with her.

That pain still sits with me to this day that we couldn't be with our mum in her grief and comfort her, no matter how complex that situation was, it was so wrong that we, as many others were at the time, were prevented from being with her.

Once our visits resumed in the outdoor accessible room we could see mum twice a week and the screen had also been replaced by a table to keep us apart and at an appropriate distance. Despite us still testing before every visit and wearing full PPE and mum was noticeably withdrawing inside herself each time we went to see her and struggled to know us. Not wanting to talk, not replying to conversation, not wanting to talk to her boys by face-time because it confused her and it looked like it caused her physical pain in her head if more than one person spoke at a time. Her eating reduced and she began to lose weight consistently by a kilo or two each week as she forgot how to eat and swallow. The nursing home carers did all they could to try and stop her losing weight but she couldn't really be bothered, it was like she had just switched off and was ready to go from this world. The only thing she would eat easily and consistently was Lindt chocolate balls or Bournville giant buttons with a grin on her face too and I can't say I blame her. I think i'd just eat chocolate too if i'd got to this point.

In December of 2021 we were told we could now allow four individual visitors into the nursing home and as we were really worried about mum's frail state we listed our boys as the two names so that they could see their grandma in person finally. My nephew lives and works in Denmark so when he came home for Christmas at the beginning of December he followed regulations and tested two days after landing and then was able to visit mum. She struggled with who he was initially but eventually recognised him and sat holding his hands and beamed from ear to ear. My Son, who lives in the USA whilst on a soccer scholarship, arrived home in the early hours of the 15th of December and dutifully two days later he completed a second Covid test which was negative and we were able to visit mum together. On our arrival mum was in the dayroom making Christmas decorations, which made me chuckle as mum was a self pronounced none artistic person. When we were kids we always knew mum was definitely of no assistance if we wanted help with Art homework. But she seemed quite happy and she did love

Christmas so I was quite happy she was enjoying herself. The carers brought mum into her bedroom to us and she smiled as she came towards us and recognised me. She looked a little confused at Jack. I said to her "Mum, I promised you that I would bring Jack to see you as soon as I was allowed and he's here for you" Unfortunately the time-lapse between July 2020, when we had special permission for Jack to see mum and dad outside before he set off to America and now, December 2021, had done it's damage. Mum didn't really know Jack was and I could see his eyes filling up as he said to me "she doesn't know who I am". I told him to just give her some time and chat to her and eventually it would come back to her. To be honest I was heartbroken for him and was willing mum to remember him. I poured us all some tea and helped mum have a couple of sips and have a chocolate or two. She kept looking between us as we chatted to her and she dropped off asleep sat in her chair holding my hand. We carried on chatting and suddenly mum woke with a bit of a start, stared at Jack intently and a beaming smile lit up her face. She grabbed at his hand and began kissing his hand and just repeated his name. He lent forward to kiss her cheek and she stroked his face smiling at him as if he was that small five year old boy again. She kept hold of his hand very tightly and nodded back off to sleep again in her chair, smiling. I was so relieved she had remembered him. We were limited to a 30 minute visit and left shortly after this with mum still napping in her chair. But she kissed us both goodbye and smiled at us knowing who we both were.

The next morning we received a call from the nursing home to say that mum wasn't too good and didn't want to get up. Which she had never done. She remained in bed and the carers noted that she didn't really have any symptoms but was complaining of her legs and knees aching. Mum did have arthritis and dementia does cause muscle pains as the limbs retract so the kept a close eye on her and she slept quite a bit. Christmas day arrived and the four of us couldn't visit mum as planned due to a potential Covid outbreak as one of the carers had tested positive but in a discussion with the carers they did say they had called an emergency doctor as mum was in more pain and they were concerned she may have an infection. The elderly are very similar to toddlers in that they can very quickly develop illnesses, being very poorly, and a couple of days of "Calpol" or in mums case antibiotics, they make an almost miraculous recovery.

The Carers actually ended up calling an ambulance due to mums pain in her hips. They were concerned she had somehow dislocated her plastic hips. She had had both replaced due to arthritis earlier in her life and pre dementia. Paramedics checked her thoroughly Christmas Day evening and said they thought it was retraction pain on the joints but didn't want to take her to hospital as it was already full within the district and she would be laid on a trolley in A and E. They advised to request an x-ray to double check all joints after Christmas in the local walk in centre to avoid A and E. They spoke with us and we were happier she was not in the hospital as she would more than likely contract Covid there and definitely not make it though to new year. They left her with pain medication and a direct dial number if things worsened and a follow up call booked with the GP for the days between Christmas and New Year. When the GP visited he thought that there was no hip issues with dislocation and agreed with the paramedics that it was retraction of the muscles. He also thought mum was at the end of her life due to her illnesses and was looking at end of life care for her but wanted to try a few days of antibiotics just to make sure that there wasn't a rogue infection that was responsible for her sudden downturn. So even though she was now in end of life care we tried several days of antibiotics but mum by this time wasn't eating and was drinking very little we were told, as we still were not allowed into the home. On the 3rd January we contacted the home and requested a call with the doctor as we were not happy that antibiotics were still being given with no improvement, if mum was near her end she needed to be as pain free as possible and without unnecessary intervention as mum had requested in her DNR (Do Not Resuscitate Order) and we as Power of Attorney had to make sure her wishes were carried out as best we could. The GP rang us and agreed that there was no change to her at all despite the antibiotics, in fact she had worsened and agreed that this was the last day of the prescription and they would not be renewed and she would be placed on full end of life care. In short this means that all unnecessary medication other than pain relief is no longer given. The good thing about this decision was that me and Louise were allowed in together to be with mum in her last days or however long she was with us. Every day we went down together, took Covid tests, dressed ourselves in full PPE and sat for hours with our mum, together. She occasionally opened her eyes and we would wet her lips with water but she mainly slept. At 6.27am on the 14th of January 2022 mum passed away peacefully and quietly while holding my hand with both of us there. She had waited to see us and her boys and then her business was done. Mum was a fighter and ultimately went in her own time at her own pace, and when she wanted to when she was ready. She died 6 days short of dad's 1st year anniversary of his death. We had lost them both within the year.

Mums funeral was everything we had been told to do by mum and was conducted by the most amazing celebrant and my friend, Helen, who also conducted dads funeral and who really brought mums character and passions very much to life. It was a day of celebrating the fact we had had our mum in our lives and that she was such a guiding force of nature. We walked in to the funeral service to Match of The Day theme tune and we walked out to The Test Match theme tune. Not what most ladies would choose but orders were orders and definitely made to be followed. Thankfully for mum we were able to have more people at the funeral and were allowed a wake, which turned into very much a celebration of mum and dad as we had been unable to have any wake at all for dad and funeral numbers were limited to 14. So a day of grieving was truly a celebration of a lifetime of achievements, memories and happy times with people who were a part of their lives and ours.

9. Moving forward

Many people offer condolences and express how awful it must be to have lost both parents within a year after caring for them both for a number of years and I can honestly say yes, it absolutely is. It is the most painful thing for anyone who has experienced it, as is any loss of a loved one. What I found as a solace was that they were both free from their illnesses and the pain it brought them.

My mum was free, free from the pain of Dementia, the most horrible death I have seen or ever want to see. I have lost friends to a few different illnesses and issues and can definitely say Dementia is one of the worst I have experienced and would never wish any family to go through what we did. You lose a loved one twice with Dementia. You are left to care for the husk of a person who you no longer know or recognise in personality. The only thing that remains is the ravaged body that resembles your loved one, while their behaviour is unrecognisable in every way. And in many cases they no longer recognise you either, which is painful every time they flinch away from you, cry at being left with you or look vacantly at you while clutching at a carer for comfort. The biggest hope I have is that in my lifetime I see a positive cure for this illness, and by positive I mean a cure that doesn't create any other suffering for those who struggle with dementia.

Or I would like to see laws to help those who suffer from illnesses such as these, that are terminal and degenerative, to be in control of their own destiny. At the very least I would like the government to actually recognise dementia for what it is and not to label it as a mental health issue. Dementia is a terminal illness, in the same way as any other terminal degenerative illness and the people who suffer from this should be given the dignity and recognition of what it actually is. Families should be able to have access to the help that they and the people who suffer really need. It should not be blocked by legislation that puts dementia in a bracket it should not be in.

Our Journey as a family and the nuances mum went through with her illness were all individual. No two people that suffer from Dementia or Alzheimer's experience the same problems and no two families that walk the path with their loved one will experience the same pain. But as with all terminal degenerative illness's you miss that loved one and every minute detail of what they were. I can definitely say I hate the pain dementia caused my beautiful mum and I hate what it put us through as a family but it definitely made us stronger and more defiant and that strength came from you mum. Always strength and always love to the last when we lost you the second and final time.

I Forget
By Louise winter

I forget I can't ring you for each day
for a chat
I forget I can't ring to say "It's
Snowing"!!
I forget I can't tell you that your cousin
has died
I forget I can't tell you your Grandson
is living his dream working as a Lego
Designer
I forget I can't tell you that your
Grandson is playing the "beautiful
game" in America
I forget I can't tell you I have a job
interview
I forget I can't ask you who's your
favourite on Strictly
I forget I can't ask you who you think
will win The Jungle
I forget I can't ask you if England won
the cricket

I forget that It's you with Dementia

I Remember When
By Louise Winter

You knew my name
You knew what I thought
You knew where things were
You knew the score
You knew how to bake
You know your favourite
You knew what was for tea

You did crosswords
You read books
You went shopping
You watched football and all sports
You wrote letters
You sent cards

You knew the actor
You knew the answer
You knew the date
You knew the alphabet
You knew the price
You knew the recipe
You knew the way

You played with your grandchildren
You took photo's

You drunk milky coffee
You were black and white not grey
You could shout
You spoke your mind

You knew your family
You knew how to knit
You knew how to teach
You knew how to sew
You knew how to catch
You knew who was lying
You knew right from wrong

You had carpets in our tent
You did hurdling for Yorkshire
You trained as a hairdresser
You grew up in Hemsworth
You went to church......then
Your learned to drive.....late

Printed in Great Britain
by Amazon